Library of
Davidson College

NORTHERN LIGHTS

 # NORTHERN LIGHTS

Poems by Susan Ludvigson

Louisiana State University Press
Baton Rouge and London 1981

Copyright © 1981 by Susan Ludvigson
All rights reserved
Manufactured in the United States of America
Designer: Patricia Douglas Crowder
Typeface: VIP Bembo
Typesetter: G&S Typesetters, Inc.

Thanks to the South Carolina Arts Commission and to the National Endowment for the Arts for a grant and a fellowship that provided time to work on some of these poems and to the MacDowell Colony and the Virginia Center for the Creative Arts, where many of these poems were written.

The author is grateful to the following periodicals for permission to reprint poems that first appeared in their pages: *Atlantic Monthly* for "On Learning That Certain Peat Bogs Contain Perfectly Preserved Bodies," copyright © 1979, by the Atlantic Monthly Company, Boston, Mass., reprinted with permission; *Epoch*; the *Georgia Review* for "The Child's Dream," "Lesson," "Motherhood," "The Psychiatrist Seeking Salvation," and "Tiwi Woman"; *Kudzu*; the *Louisville Review*; *Mississippi Review*; the *Nation* for "All I Ever Wanted Was a God," "Trying to Change the Subject," and "The Wisdom"; the *Ohio Review*; *Open Places* (Spring, 1980, Issue No. 29) for "Good Child," "Margaret," and "The Kiss"; the *Paris Review*; *Pembroke Magazine*; *Pieces*; the *Pikestaff Review*; *Poetry* for "The Widow"; *South Carolina Review* (Clemson University); *Southern Poetry Review*; the *Southern Review*; *Unwharrie Review*. "The Quarrel" first appeared in *Porch*; "Trying to Change the Subject" also appeared in *Bear Crossings*, New South Publications, 1978; "The Child's Dream" is included in the 1980 *Anthology of Magazine Verse and Yearbook of American Poetry*, and "The Widow" and "Motherhood" in the 1981 edition of that anthology; Part 3 of *Northern Lights* was published as a pamphlet in the Inland Boat Series, Porch Publications, 1980, under the title *The Wisconsin Women*.

LIBRARY OF CONGRESS CATALOGING IN PUBLICATION DATA

Ludvigson, Susan.
  Northern lights.
  I. Title.
PS3562.U27N6   811'.54   81-6039
ISBN 0-8071-0879-0   AACR2
ISBN 0-8071-0880-4 (pbk.)

For my son Joel and for my mother and in memory of my father

Contents

PART ONE

- 3 Lesson
- 4 Corn
- 5 In the Beginning
- 6 To a Playmate, Accused
- 7 The Punishment
- 8 Romance
- 9 Little Women
- 10 Burials
- 11 Tale for a Daughter
- 12 Motherhood
- 13 Absolution
- 15 Again, Father, That Dream
- 16 The Child's Dream
- 17 Good Child
- 18 Trainer's Temper Bars Him from His Beloved Elephants
- 20 On Learning That Certain Peat Bogs Contain Perfectly Preserved Bodies
- 21 Tiwi Woman
- 23 The Quarrel
- 24 Swazi Bride
- 25 The Ladies of Skill and Daring
- 26 Elephant Act at the Family Circus
- 27 The Kiss
- 28 Search Party
- 29 A Story
- 30 The Woman Who Keeps Fish
- 31 Jeanne d'Arc
- 32 The Widow
- 34 The Psychiatrist Seeking Salvation

PART TWO

- 37 A Few of the Women
- 37 Anne
- 37 Alice and Frances

38	Emma
38	Edith
39	Sylvia
40	Margaret
41	Mary
42	First Wife, Eleanor, Missing Five Years, Presumed Dead
43	Victoria
45	Wilma
46	Minnie
47	Etta

PART THREE

51	Reading Between the Words
52	Explaining It
53	A Romance
54	Breasts
55	Some Uses of Art
56	The Artist to Her Patron
57	After Choosing Against Them
58	A Bargain at Any Price
59	Country Living
60	All I Ever Wanted Was a God
61	All My Orifices Are Too Small
62	Trying to Change the Subject
63	Alliances
64	Listening
65	Deceptions
66	Fear in New Hampshire
67	Your Letter
68	How Many Women Do You Pass Each Day?
69	Trying to Make Light of Our Loneliness
70	Things We Can't Prepare For
71	The Wisdom

 ONE

Lesson

My father said quicksand
might be hidden in the tall swamp-grass,
would suck me down, down
to the center of earth.
Even in fall, the dry season,
when the horses snapped reeds
with each step,
a fearful swarm of insects
could mean that pit,
wet as fresh manure, was only disguised,
leaves covering it over like a blind.
Mother, no Ceres, did not believe
I would disappear. Watch
for blackbirds, she said,
handing me the old wicker basket.
Wherever they land is safe.
Bring me the small blue flowers
that grow close to the ground
and the tallest cattails
you can find.
I followed those redwings in
feeling like Gretel, whistling for courage.
When I came out,
a mass of cattails over my shoulder
like a bag of gold,
basket filled with blossoms,
she was waiting at the edge,
waving and smiling.

Corn

My mother thought the silk
would make us beautiful.
She wound it through her fingers
whispering the names of her sisters
like a prayer.
My sister understood:
while the two of them giggled together,
I shucked and put the water on.
And as I chewed the rows across,
they worked their way around,
slowly turning each buttery ear
to their delicate mouths.

The stalks were thick enough
to lean against,
and in a forest of them
making the only shade,
I dreamed of my young aunts
dancing, calling the rain.

In the Beginning

The day she began to cry, ironing,
I sat in a square of light
on the kitchen floor
learning to print my name.
I remember the *S*
kept coming out backward.
In tears, one hand clenching a shirt,
she bent to draw me a letter,
then forgot me and wept for hours.

As the sun moved higher
my linoleum spot changed shape,
elongated, until
the paper's edge would not fit
to its rim.

I listened, studied,
in shadow, then in dark,
forming that one imperfect word.

To a Playmate, Accused

Each time you went to your grandmother's
to live, weeks and months at a time,
we said we remembered kerosene
in the garage, and strange smells
on your clothes. When you came home
and spoke of saints, whose faces
glowed for you in the sky,
we fingered your rosary, whispered
of other mysteries we knew
you could conjure.
Once I dreamed your red hair
brightened my window like the moon,
and when I woke, hearing sirens,
it was proof.

We held a trial.
Someone testified to matches
under your rug. Another saw you
brush soot from your jacket.
I said I knew you since you were born,
had watched your eyes light up
unnaturally at birthdays,
always claiming more years
than you had.

The next time they sent you away
we waved good-bye, trembling,
joyous with fear.

You laughed, your voice
crackling like dry leaves.

The Punishment

Remember the tree, Charlie?
Where I tied you with ropes
wound from your shoulders
all the way down
to your skinny ankles
like a loose-wrapped mummy?
And then took the branches
lying on the ground
and stuffed them
between you and the ropes
like jail bars,
not to help hold you in,
but to scratch you?
Weeks earlier, Grandma told me
you went to the hospital
with a broken arm,
claiming I did it
because you tried to kiss me.
I would have,
but that's not how it happened
and I've always been a fiend
for truth.
You cried, but not enough,
so I took another leafy branch
and whipped you. And when
I finally turned you loose,
the welts blossoming
on your arms and legs
like roses,
your tears did not move me
at all. I could still see you
at the emergency room
grinning, arm in a sling,
selling stories to the nurses
that sent them out laughing,
repeating my innocent name.

Romance

I'm back on that street
where at midnight Jeff and Barry
become Batman and Robin.
We make toothpowder bombs, store them
in a secret place at the river,
where we aren't allowed.
Each evening at eight
(an hour after my bedtime)
the neighborhood kids have a game,
boys against girls.
I listen to someone get caught
and kissed
under my window—
the sound of an oar
dipped into the lake.
When finally I fall asleep
I dream the back yard stretches
to the river itself, a field
full of snakes and traps.
I find myself on a ferris wheel,
hands gripping the bar
and hanging, until the wheel turns,
and I wake, suspended over the water.

Little Women

There in the playhouse
making pies of flour and water
and apples from the neighbor's yard,
we learned to handle anything—
husbands who stopped in
just long enough
to sample the cookies,
gardens that washed away
in the first spring storm,
and babies crying,
their mechanical wails
stuck in their throats
like dimes. Sometimes
we thought we'd try something
else—I'd be
a missionary in Africa,
and a ballet dancer,
and go to Mars.
I remember standing on the sidewalk,
hands raised to the sky,
proclaiming *I* would not
be married, have children,
live in a neighborhood
like this. But always
we returned
to the little house
behind my real one,
put on the long dresses
with folds that wrapped us
like gifts,
the shiny high heels,
and the feathered hats.
Then we practiced
a dignified walk
around and around the block.

Burials

The difficulties of hiding anything.
How for a child, it all seems easy.
I had a room behind my room,
a space back of the built-in drawers
next to the closet. I could
take a drawer out, crawl through,
and ease it back like a piece
in a puzzle. With a flashlight,
books, the world was safe as Freiberg
before the war.
I kept my valuables there:
cigar boxes full of bottle caps
(worth money then—some kind of contest),
a pile of comics, the antique china doll
whose legs and arms I snapped one day
for spite.

Today I look through a notebook.
It has my name, but I know
none of this. Some of the words
I can't define, and books I discuss
I don't remember reading.
The writing is small and neat
like my aunt's. It almost draws pictures.

Sometimes even my face is a surprise.
I walk out happy, but someone comes up
on the street and asks what's wrong.
I think of last night's dream:
my father alive again at the table,
a baby crying, pages falling from the sky
like rain, and then like leaves
needing to be raked, put in order.
I can see which way the signs point,
but who would want to go there?

Tale for a Daughter

We knew what cold was. Each morning Dad rode a horse to the auction barn at the edge of town, then walked the rest of the way to work. After school I'd meet him at the shop, and when he finished sweeping up, we half-ran (my long strides matching his) the mile or so to where he'd left the gray, whose mane and forelock by then were ice, like foil you hang on a Christmas tree. When he pulled me up behind him, the horse dancing a circle on the slippery road, I became a Norwegian pioneer, romantic and tough like my grandmother. All the way home my mittened hands, clasped round my father's middle, felt ready to crack, to break off at the wrists like an electric cord snaps at 40 below when you touch it. Behind his wide back that blocked the wind, my face and body were warmer, and the horse's heat as we galloped spread into my thighs, teaching me early what women must learn, one way or another, about survival.

Motherhood

Think of gentleness, as when
a head lifts and nods to a child,
easy permission. I remember
going back and forth to the kitchen
in winter, where the oven held us
like small lovely moths to the light.
Mother would hand us warm bread
with jelly, and we'd flit away
until we were cold again.

Now all my gestures are lost.
Too late for a bowl of cookies,
a hug, to make any difference.
He's younger in my dreams,
sometimes a brother. I walk out
to the barn to find the mare
I love, to give it to him.
But he can't understand,
and thinks she's dangerous.

I would begin again, have children
late, when I've learned
not to rely on words, but on
bread rising each Saturday
in a life that would stay
as firm as a boy's deliberate stride
onto the soccer field.
I'd know what can be forgiven,
what grace warms the air like steam.

Absolution

for my sister

Like our father, drugged at the end,
his own blue eyes
blinking away the visions,
Uncle Earl was a caught fox,
furious and pleading.
Strapped in the bed,
the snakes fighting for him again,
he didn't know you, and you
wouldn't claim him. Death,
when it came, was not quick,
but unexpected, as for all the wicked
we think will never die.

The nurses laughed, their voices
floating above him like a song,
a chant he couldn't hear the words to.
He cried out once for his sisters
who, when they speak of him,
remember how their mother
saved months for a billiard table
to lure him home,
and when she got it,
put it in the living room,
disgracing them.
Even then the bottles piled up
like coral, sharp and poisonous,
half alive.

He came home with us once
after Mother found him
sprawled in a car, his face
a web of wrinkles, dirt, and tears.
The first time I ever saw
a man's whole body tremble.
For hours we listened to him
lecture himself
while she cried and made coffee,

pot after pot, and drank it with him
through the solemn night.

Now you remember only
passing the closed door
to his room
where the shrieks
could not be restrained
like arms and legs,
but scraped the air raw.
In your white dress, you
and everyone in the place
were immune.

But now he appears,
a disease of the blood,
disguised.

You think your guilt is for
our father, whose last days
went on forever
while you rubbed his legs
and turned him,
smoothed the cracked skin with lotion,
the terror with your voice.

The same hospital.

The same loss, a slicing away
of breath
no matter what you did
or didn't do.

Again, Father, That Dream

      Leading the saddled pony back
      to find its frightened rider, I see
      a cafe, drift in for a cup of coffee.
      Those plain white porcelain mugs
      undo me again, I cannot drink
      or have a conversation
      without the sound of your voice
      calling *Mabel, Mabel* into the kitchen,
      Mother coming out, shy and hesitant,
      hiding her spattered apron
      with her hands. I hear you
      whistling, that warble
      rising on the air of this strange
      place like finches suddenly let in.
      The others do not notice.
      The radio comes on, a ballgame,
      and I remember the pony, tied
      outside, far from the lost child.

The Child's Dream

If I could start my life again,
I'd keep the notebook
I promised myself at nine—
a record of all the injustice
done by adults: that accusing tone
when they speak, the embarrassments
before relatives, like the time
I had to put on my swimsuit in the car
while Mother chatted with an uncle
who peered in, teasing.
And *wouldn't* they be sorry
later, when they read it,
after I'd been run over by a truck,
their faces darkening
like winter afternoons.
And I, of course (if I survived),
would have a reminder,
in my own hand,
so I'd be the perfect parent,
my children radiant as the northern lights.
It's like poems you hope
will be read by someone who knows
they're for him, and cry
at what he did or didn't do,
wishing to touch your face once more,
to cradle your body.
You can almost hear what he'd tell you
with his voice that sounds
like the sea rolling in
over and over, like a song.

Good Child

*I am concerned that when you leave here today your daughter will go crazy again.
And I think the reason she will do it is to save your marriage.*
from an article by Janet Malcolm in *The New Yorker*

>Now the slightest touch of the breeze
>to a branch, the rattle of leaves
>on my window, and the glass gets
>brittle, threatens to disintegrate.
>The piano plays itself in my dreams,
>always a frenzied tune,
>and voices of friends have turned
>animal, my fear making them
>vicious, bullying. When I speak
>Mother does not hear the words
>at all, but Father locks himself
>away. I find old letters I wrote
>from camp, letters they saved
>in the desk drawer. I rewrite them
>telling the truth: I am not
>having fun. Each day the lake
>gets deeper, and my breath
>no stronger. I dive for rocks
>covered in tinfoil, but when
>I come up, my hands are empty,
>the others win the prizes.
>Today I walked the lane
>to our old house.
>The trees were down in the coming wind
>and I could hear hail before it fell.

Trainer's Temper Bars Him from His Beloved Elephants

Headline, the Charlotte *Observer*

All day when one is giving birth
you sweat, roll on the ground,
clenching your knees to your belly.
At night you lie beside her
groaning, as she bellows pain,
humiliation, to the stars.
You understand the language.
When you sleep on the ground
you feel it shudder
with the memory of a herd
turning the grassy plain
to dust. When you bring straw
you want to spin it gold,
to make vast brocade blankets
and a shimmering jacket for yourself.

But when the youngest refuses
to eat, you smash the bottle
on his soft head, claiming
an accident. Sometimes
when they cry all night
for nothing, you take a fat stick
and let them know whose word
is law. They never blame you,
but tremble in the corners
while you croon.

Your father wept
each time he bruised you.
Once you went to school
with a broken arm
and when you got home
he twisted it, so you'd
remember. When he died
you stayed at the grave
five days in the rain,
still hearing his words:

We're all beasts, son.
Trust no one.
Do not marry.
Do not have children.
Nobody understands
the nature of love.

On Learning That Certain Peat Bogs Contain Perfectly Preserved Bodies

Under this town's ashes
lies a man, still sweating
the long summer days,
his body
perfect as morning,
even to the bacon and eggs
in his belly.
His skin is damp
in the humid earth,
closed eyes heavier
under rain.
The heart quit pumping early,
but when a rock eases down
and cuts an arm
or grazes his back,
blood still seeps
from the veins,
the clots blooming
like poppies around him.
In the brain
memories lie opened,
one into the other:
the crunch of the ax
as he swings down hard,
his wife calling him in,
a woman singing his name
in the distance.
He does not hear them,
but they are there,
claiming their portions.
By now the wife may be
dead too, the ax passed down
to his son, or rusted
under the woodpile.
The woman cannot recall
her own clear voice
or the features of the man
who should be bones.

Tiwi Woman

Whenever a man dies and his widow remarries, the personal names given to her children by the dead man become taboo, and the new husband provides the children with new names. Because of a unique betrothal system, young girls usually marry middle-aged or old men, resulting in many widows, who are required to remarry immediately at each husband's death.
Hart and Pilling, The Tiwi of North Australia

>When I was Lily
>I was very small.
>Mother said my legs
>must not carry me
>beyond the twisted tree
>at the riverbank,
>I should wish
>that my skin become
>like petals,
>should rub my body
>with oils,
>sing bird songs
>under the open sky.
>
>When I became Lark
>I braided my hair
>with leaves
>and striped feathers,
>took my betrothed
>to the clearing
>I'd made with my sister
>deep in the forest. There
>under the darkening sky
>he stroked my thighs
>as if I were golden.
>That night
>my whole life
>opened to the moon.
>
>Now I am Summer.
>Always the heat finds me
>under a thatched roof.

One by one, husbands
burn in my flesh,
carving new seasons,
transforming
all the birds
I love
and the flowers.

The Quarrel

Implicit in Semai thinking about punan *is the idea that to make someone unhappy, especially by frustrating that person's desires, will increase the probability of the distressed person's having an accident that will cause physical injury.*
Robert Knox Dentan, *The Semai*

> She walks among the women
> sighing, her small breasts
> crossed with a dozen strands
> of beads, her dark hair
> bright with flowers.
> When she spills a pot
> of cooking rice,
> burning her hands,
> her soft cries are like birds
> trapped in the darkened hut.
>
> The women shake their heads.
>
> Somewhere a young man
> is hunting, his darts
> poisoned with upas sap
> and toadskin. His marksmanship
> is proven, but today
> his hands tremble,
> guilt washes over him
> like rain,
> he cannot kill the quail.

Swazi Bride

In one of the most dramatic moments of the ritual, the girl stands in the cattle byre of her husband, mourning in song the loss of her girlhood freedom and crying to her brothers to rescue her from her fate.
Hilda Kuper, The Swazi

    Soon they will come
    to take me. I cannot
    do this, my mouth is filled
    with dust, with the airborne
    hair of cattle drifting around me
    like clouds. Breathing,
    I taste my death, and swallow it.
    Keep the child from me,
    it is no wish of mine
    to grow big in the belly
    like someone starving.
    I *would* starve. A man
    cannot want a wife who chooses
    her family's hut,
    whose eyes hold the antelope's
    terror. This song is real,
    my flesh grows cold
    as the stream amid these warm
    bodies calling, under this
    hunting moon. Do not
    come near me with that
    red earth, my blood
    will not flow for you,
    I keep myself locked
    like Christian doors,
    I want no cow, no promises,
    no sister to help ease the pain.

The Ladies of Skill and Daring

Three sisters leap onto three enormous
colored balls. They dance, their feet
curved to caress the surface, as if
to assure it, to keep it smooth. Now
the spheres move under them slightly
like animals curled into sleep,
dreaming these dark-haired girls.
All three wind slowly
up a high ramp
where together they nearly fall.
But they are graceful, they twist
their sequined bodies in the air
until they are still
as blackbirds on telephone wire.
They give the breathless audience
what it wants: the beauty of risk
in unison, all the while keeping
their women's secrets between them
like a balance pole.

Elephant Act at the Family Circus

The hefty girl strains,
pulls herself to the elephant's head,
one arm outstretched, the way
she'd climb a hay wagon, that hand
clutching a pitchfork.
Now she lifts both her hands
to the air, her smile fixed,
and I can almost see a drift
of grain slipping through her fingers,
see her become a child,
mouth and body relaxed,
sliding down a haystack
to the arms of a boy.
But she stands
on the elephant's back
instead, still imploring.
They circle the ring again and again
as the children cheer.
Finally he wraps his trunk around her,
lifts her down gently
like a lover.
When she takes her last bow
on the ground,
she is the farmer's young wife,
she has just won a prize
for her bull at the county fair.

The Kiss

A mother of two is so allergic to the bite of an inch-long insect called the kissing bug, she faces death unless someone starts producing more antigen (a liquid medicine made from the bugs) to counteract the bites. For the present, research money has run out.
Los Angeles *Times*

> She does not hear him
> ascend the leg of her bed
> as if it were a mountain
> where at the top, only at the top,
> the sweetest berries grow.
>
> He is relentless as a child
> who could wait all morning in silence
> piling and unpiling blocks in the corner
> for a reward like this.
>
> He stops a moment, puffs his small
> pink belly as the bed trembles
> with her breathing.
>
> Finally he slips
> into the fragrant sheets
> and waits for a smooth breast
> to flatten on its side
> as she shifts position.
> Some of his brothers
> were frozen alive,
> their bodies dissolved even now,
> perhaps, in her blood.
>
> But it is not revenge he is after.
>
> He wants only to taste her,
> to feel his power
> swell with her fear, to sing
> the song of her life.

Search Party

It is believed that a dermoid, a tumor made up of skin tissue, sometimes having hair and teeth, may be the remnant of a woman's undeveloped twin.

Experts have been called in
to explore the territory,
to look for the dead, the missing.
It is rumored that my sister
lies somewhere within,
breathless, blind, dark hair
fallen over ravaged skin,
netting a twisted body.

Spinning their silver drills,
they cut through debris
to find the tunnels, now caving
and dangerous. Oh, they are impressive,
they know their way around.
These structures are all the same:
the supports weaken in similar places,
and the skilled do not need blueprints
to know where somebody is likely
to be pinned, or how to follow
a bloody trail. In their
asbestos uniforms, their hard hats,
they can move quickly, safe,
along collapsing walls.

When they come out, victorious,
the foreman reports,
she was there, all right,
curled like any victim
into herself, barely recognizable
after all these years.

A Story

He remembers how his mother used to stand at the window for hours, humming to herself as if she were happy. He'd go in and out the screen door making just enough noise to draw her attention, not make her angry. But when she turned her head back, he'd think of a small deer testing the air in a clearing where everything only seemed safe. Sometimes he'd go to his own room upstairs to study the view. All he'd ever see were the fields of corn, the pond, and dust rising like swarms of bees when a car passed on the road.

Later, after he'd grown, he found the letters she must have written every day for years. "Dearest," one said, "Today your face came in a cloud like a saint's. I could see your scowl billow and shift to a grin when I held the child up high and pointed to a bird's nest in the oak." Another: "Love, I canned 3 dozen quarts of peaches, 10 pounds of tomatoes, enough string beans to last all winter and then some. But you'd think I hadn't anything to eat, I'm thin as cane again." The letters were not addressed; no name appeared in her clear hand anywhere.

When she died, and his father didn't weep, but spread the ashes over the garden as she'd asked, he went to the kitchen and stared through the same clean window. Hearing a flock of geese in the distance, he waited for the V to pass over, squawking. Instead, they dropped silent as swans into the empty front yard. The way the sun hit them, he almost thought they were golden.

The Woman Who Keeps Fish

Even asleep I hear any change
in the air bubbling from the tanks.
Today everything's right. See how the angels
grow and grow, always healthy?
Their small bodies ripple the world
softly, like leaves.
I could name them, but if you care
you'll learn for yourself how to call them.
Notice the iridescence of that group.
In deeper, colder waters, they brighten
their way through the moonless nights.
Only a few survive. But here
I chart their safer lives each day.
I know who eats, and how many swipes
that one takes at his brother.
I know who's eager to mate, and how
to encourage romance among the shy.

Though I love them, I'm not sentimental.
If one dies by accident, or someone's
overfeeding, I get angry.
But if I choose war
to please the restless bettas (look,
one's red as the August sun
right now, and flaring—another,
in that bowl, turns teal to smoky black,
his fierce head getting darker),
I know what I risk.

How often you come here
depends. Can you distinguish
male from female in this pair?
Do you detect her swollen body,
his careful indifference?
Are you sensitive to temperature?
To color?
Do you swim?

Jeanne d'Arc

To be chosen—

my small body rejoices
at the words,
encases itself in silver
more lovely than silk.

Not to stay in the village
and marry the miller,
his babies heavy in my arms
as loaves of bread—

not to be God's bride
dressed in the long black robe
I've secretly named a shroud,
needing always to chasten myself
for my shimmering dreams—

but Christ's innocent mistress,
Lily of war!

Still, I can scarcely believe
how each time I speak
the sky brightens.

When the voice first came
from behind the dark trees
I sat for a long time, trembling.
Now my skin
burns, imagining how it will be,
the horse between my thighs,
a thousand men behind me
singing.

The Widow

A stranger arrives at her door
in a T-shirt, his truck
parked outside like a sign:
This is an honest repairman.
He wants directions, but she
does not know the street.
When he asks to use the phone,
she lets him into the kitchen
where the water has just begun
to boil, steaming the windows
like breath.

She remembers the novel
where a man holds a knife
to a child's small throat,
drawing a thin line of blood,
then takes the young mother
off in his truck to rape her.
She thinks where her knives are,
imagines throwing the water
straight from the stove
in his face.

He murmurs something
into the phone.
She has gone to another room
and can't make out the words,
the tone is too soft,
but she hears the water
boil over, spatter the gleaming
stainless steel of her range
like the hiss of firecrackers
before they explode.
He pulls the pan off the burner,
calls to her,
Lady? Lady?

She hides in the bathroom,
listens, even after she hears

the door open again, and close
like the click of a trigger.
When at last the truck
pulls away, she comes out,
spends the whole afternoon
drifting back and forth
to the window.

Making supper,
she burns her hand,
cries softly
long after the pain is gone.

The next morning, she's amazed
to see she'd forgotten
to lock the back door,
to turn off the lights
that burned all night
in the kitchen.

The Psychiatrist Seeking Salvation

He enters the office
in darkness, seeing the faces
of patients in stars
through a window. Like a thief
he points his flashlight
into a file, where his own words
light up. His fingers
are awkward, thumbing through these lives
he knows so well, but he
goes on. He takes out the tapes,
is more bold now, plays
one after the other softly,
humming between them, as he
removes each cartridge
and replaces it. Now he lights
a candle, lies down
to watch the flame,
anxious for light to begin
outside. When he falls asleep
he dreams of stars endlessly burning
and of new rooms painted white
without plants or paintings or secrets.

 TWO

The poems in this section were inspired by Michael Lesy's *Wisconsin Death Trip*, which consists of a series of news clippings and photographs from a small town newspaper, the *Badger State Banner*, around the turn of the century.

A Few of the Women

from photographs

Anne

There you sit sleeping at the piano.
Your daughter is bored
and ashamed, your husband
clearly disgusted. Even one of the pictures
hangs askew, as if your drowsing contempt
takes in everything, lets it all
wait for a better hour.
I remember you when
you ironed the underwear
and your house could have been used
for commercials: Anne's whiter
than virgin laundry. What happens
when a woman produces
a plain, untalented child,
and the lines in her husband's face
get sharper, the cushions thin?
Annie always had gumption, they said,
but they didn't see your slack body
there, at the piano,
at three in the afternoon.

Alice and Frances

In hammocks with the boys
you look content:
idyllic summer afternoon
by the lake, the trees
holding you suspended.
But you are
the ugliest sisters in Racine
and you know
these handsome lads
didn't come for the picnic
though you prepared the perfect
chicken, potato salad, pies.

37

As the sun smooths the lake
to copper, one by one
they will take you
to the shack down the road
where you will give them each
the Fourth of July.

Emma

She was almost three
when you propped her in the casket
by the door. It took two days
of staying up till dawn
to make the dress, but she
is perfect, serene,
hand clasped to her heart,
a rose by her waist, hollyhock doll
at her head.
Ben can bring the neighbors in now.
You have strong coffee ready.
You know the men must get to the fields
by noon, this won't last long.
Though you have not wept today
your eyes feel swollen,
you can scarcely keep them open.

Edith

It doesn't matter
that your hair's a mess,
the puff of your sleeves
gone soft. You look past the cabin
where your father lugs the wood in,
yells Hurry, the snow is coming fast.
You still see your lover's ship at Ålesund,
high walls of rock,
land slicing into the sea.
You watch the tall waves lift
a confusion of wood and spray.

Your dark eyes stay amazed
through all the long cold months.

Sylvia

Your whole face is pleasure
as you slip those gorgeous snakes
around your throat.
Who knocked over the bench,
the kid who ran up and dumped them
in your lap?
You got the last laugh though,
you with your Sunday hat
still straight,
now arranging your blouse
with glistening necklaces
that twist and swell in the sun.

Margaret

Mrs. A. J. Cowles, aged 87 years, died at Beloit. She had been married to Deacon Cowles, who survives her, for nearly 68 years. On the occasion of her last birthday her eccentric husband presented her with a coffin which he had made with his own hands and in which she was buried.
March 16, 1893, the *Badger State Banner*

All these months I've polished it
with good wax, made him see
I loved the smooth grain,
the rich finish.
I'd been too well to think of it
as bed, but at the first ache
he removed the plants I'd put on top.
Now, lying here, seeing it open,
I try to admire the well-sealed joints,
the whorled pattern on the inside lid,
but I am irritable, ungrateful.
I pray, but God must know.
Last night I dreamed
I locked myself in the pantry.
The neighbors tried to let me out
but the spring floods came
and they all left in boats.
This morning
the pain is no worse than ever
but I keep drowsing off
and I wake up crying.

Mary

Mary Ricks, the Wisconsin window-smasher, has put in an appearance at Eau Claire. She was taken into custody by a policeman as she was about to wreck a fine plate glass window.
February 22, 1894, the *Badger State Banner*

> It was *so clean*. Mother used to say,
> if you polish one like that
> a man might walk through it,
> thinking it a clear passage
> to the garden, but be surprised
> by the crack and the instantaneous
> shock of something slicing his shoulder,
> his belly, so that the blood
> would run from here to Lake Michigan.
> Sometimes I stand outside a greenhouse.
> Cardinals batter themselves
> on the roof, the sides.
> Sometimes I find a sparrow
> with a broken neck, but never
> any blood. Mother was wrong.
> Nobody bleeds but me.
> I try to wait till after dark
> on the main streets,
> but when I can't, someone
> always comes too soon. Still,
> I have plenty of scars,
> and in jail they bring bandages,
> are usually gentle with wounds.

First Wife, Eleanor, Missing Five Years, Presumed Dead

At Sheboygan, a mysterious woman dressed in black and wearing a heavy dark veil enticed from school George Alfred Preston and Hattie May Preston, aged respectively 11 and 9 years, children of George Preston. The children were hurried away in a carriage which started in a northerly direction, supposedly for Plymouth, where a train could be taken.
December 30, 1897, the Badger State Banner

> That winter he was good to me,
> it's true, and not his fault
> she died. He used to bring me
> honey and tea in the morning,
> and when the sun came
> into the kitchen
> he'd carry me there, prop my feet
> on a bench near the stove.
> When he went out to cut more wood
> I'd watch, admiring the skill,
> his easy walk across the yard.
> I remember how the light
> changed shape on the floor,
> how I knew how long he'd be
> by the shifting patterns.
> I *did* rest the whole time
> like the doctor said
> but when the baby came
> and didn't last two weeks
> I had to go away.
> All those years in Milwaukee
> I waited for him,
> keeping Catherine's house
> and reading the Bible.
> God meant you to be a mother,
> she told me,
> and that night
> as I bathed her Elizabeth,
> I had a sign.

Victoria

Victoria Hanna, a middle-aged woman of Kaukauna, Outgamie County, was bound over to Commissioner Bloodgood the other day in the sum of $500 on the charge of sending obscene matter through the mails. The woman had a spite against a neighbor and mailed her a letter of the filthiest description.
May 14, 1885, the *Badger State Banner*

    Dear Mrs. Anderson,

    Your Lars came to my house again
    last night, wearing his dung overalls,
    and when I heard him brush the hedge
    under my window, I sent out the dog.
    You think I make this up because
    you have hair like my sister Bertie,
    but I tell you, he's here
    more than twice a week.
    Sometimes I pretend I don't know.
    I slip my chemise off
    slowly, as if I'm so weary
    I can hardly stretch my arms.
    (And in the moonlight I know
    how white my skin is,
    how lean, even now, my body.)
    Sometimes I complain of the heat
    and pull everything off,
    stretch on the bed,
    my legs and arms flung wide,
    wishing aloud for a fan
    or someone to fan me.
    Then I get up
    and dust myself, breast to toe,
    with strawberry talcum.

    I always hear the swish of leaves outside.

    But last night I got tired
    of the game, tired of your tolerant smile
    every time you see me.
    This time, just check the right leg
    of his barn pants.

I can see you sitting there
in your parlor,
your thin lips drawn
to a line as straight as the seam
you'll sew. You with your
snaky black hair.
You with your pity.

Wilma

Mrs. Phillip Fredericks, aged 82 years, who was partly insane, threw herself in her neighbor's cistern at Beloit and was drowned. She had long planned death in this manner.
July 23, 1891, the Badger State Banner

>I waited for summer.
>Easier to get me out, and mostly,
>the garden is going good.
>The corn's half up,
>plenty of beans for Helen already,
>and the preacher's back from his sister's.
>I can't think when I've felt so fine.
>It's like the time Phillip took us
>to Madison. It rained two weeks
>and we had to take John and Nathan,
>but they behaved.
>We found every kind of mushroom,
>and when the boys took sick
>there was a doctor not a mile away.
>We did everything—
>stayed up all night
>with cool rags for their heads,
>took turns carrying pails.
>When it was over, Phillip and I
>came back alone.
>Helen's boy was by to check on the peas
>yesterday, so he won't come now.
>It's hot, but that's better than thunder.
>No sign of storm.

Minnie

Miss Minnie Rose of Beaver Dam shot herself in the Plankinton House in Milwaukee. She left a letter in which she asks that her body be destroyed by electricity. . . . In the letter she says that untrue stories circulated about her drove her to suicide.
December 29, 1898, the *Badger State Banner*

> I wanted the same room
> on the fourth floor,
> the one in the corner
> with the oak by the window,
> but it was taken.
> I'd planned to sit
> in the green velvet chair
> where he held me on his lap,
> said I shocked him with my tongue.
> All that talk of hot wires
> and currents and volts
> he said I made him feel,
> I began to think I was dangerous.
> Shouldn't touch you
> when I'm wet, I said,
> and he laughed and laughed,
> the dark hairs on his arms
> almost crackling.
>
> He should have been a stranger
> riding from town to town
> through the worst summer storms,
> not plain old Ruth Peterson's husband,
> who died pinned under a wagon.

Etta

Etta Walker, the girl who disappeared the other day from Boscobel on the eve of her marriage, was found at 2 o'clock the next morning but could give no account of herself, being in a completely dazed condition. Fred Stahel, who was to have married her, would not fulfill his engagement.
April 24, 1890, the *Badger State Banner*

>Violets and trilliums
>began filling the lawn,
>crept out of the woods
>in an hour,
>so that the whole yard
>was purple and white
>before sunset: flowers
>hung from the trees,
>wrapped around my old bicycle
>there by the fence,
>and the porch swing grew deep
>with petals.
>When I walked,
>even the smallest, most delicate
>stems were not crushed,
>but sent out new shoots
>that opened to instant blossoms.
>
>At bedtime I couldn't sleep
>and I went to the forest.
>When I came out,
>my arms and legs
>were a garden of bruises,
>everything else had gone brown.

THREE

Reading Between the Words

Today I take out your letters.
The words bump into each other
as the story clatters on. At the end
of a line you run out of space.
Your comma or period leaps to the next
, as you rush to tell me how you think
of her, of me. You are speaking of storms,
the vast black clouds as you drive,
lightning breaking her face
into thousands of fissures, fraying her hair.
You remember me lying on a sofa, watching
the valley transform in the sky's
white splitting. A sheet from another
year: tight voiced, she instructs in the gallery,
the grocery store, nursery. You go to the woods,
alone. You hear childhood noises cracking
your sleep like glass. You were afraid
of walking. Once cut into intricate patterns,
your feet wear thick boots. You write
of the first bad year, and the last. Now
your paragraphs merge. There is no space.
Even the postmark tells: too close to come
by air, something always too close.

Explaining It

After that I fell in love with the photographer.
Stand here, and here, he said, ordering me.
I knew it was all right to take direction
because he understood me perfectly, which side
to catch, how to camouflage wrinkles, scars,
pain, malaise, memories of men with rough hands.
I loved him because he could see everything,
and seeing me, knew where all the shadows
would fall. Turn your face to the light,
he'd say, and suddenly my skin would be
translucent. He could remake me in an instant,
my body like a bride's, my eyes shining
with surprise and innocence.

A Romance

For me the body was always a garden of flowers covered by nice skin.
Artur Rubinstein

        My legs are dreaming
        of a new life. Each day
        I stretch in the ballet room,
        hearing the muscles sigh,
        "More, I can do more,"
        pleased at so much attention.
        Even when small groans
        escape from behind the knees
        where they try to hide,
        the thighs continue to blush,
        undaunted. These are legs
        I cried for at thirteen,
        sitting in the bathtub,
        asking God please to make them
        just *average*. How I hated them,
        skinny as pine, disdaining
        their length, their whiteness.
        Now, at mid-life, the body
        learns to love itself,
        that pale orchid still unfolding.
        Soon each tendon will turn
        its ear to the music,
        summer will blossom with dance.

Breasts

The first time they mattered
I was eleven, drying the dishes,
when my little brother
folded me into a chair
with a jab—
a pain so deep I knew
he'd stopped my heart.
That was before I'd even noticed
them growing. Later, wishing
them large as moons, I treasured
their tenderness,
pressed the swollen sides
with my fingers, the way
I love now, you firming the flesh
as a sculptor fondles soft clay.
When did I learn the pleasure
of one entirely embraced by a hand,
nippling the palm,
the other begging?
As you enter the room, they grow warm,
lift toward the sun like small flowers.
I follow, their sure direction
taking us somewhere we've been.
Again, something stops my breath
like a fist, but the heart
knows its part, does not frighten me now
with its long, deliberate pause.

Some Uses of Art

Yes, the camera.
I'll photograph your shoulder,
the smallest lines on your wrist,
one muscular thigh. Men
rarely feel beautiful,
I understand. But you will discover
your exquisite features
in my eye:
the angle of your torso,
bent, the flexed knee,
a silhouette of chin.

Enlarged, matted, they'll
be abstractions,
unrecognizable to strangers
as closeups of rain
or particles of leaves
veined like skin.

Each night, in secret,
your parts will leave their frames,
the leg will straighten
and shake itself loose,
the tongue moisten,
the chest, that silvery field,
sigh as I take you in.

The Artist to Her Patron

You like it best when I draw
the world bloody. Any source—
the place where I sliced my leg
shaving this morning, the baby's
eye after an explosion of tears,
the clot in the mare's throat
near the end, when nobody knows
why her breath is so short—
gives you pleasure.
I could buy fresh meat
and cut it, leave the drippings
in a glass, as a simple reminder,
could even use that liquid
mixed with paint
for a brighter effect. I too
have always loved the color
deep as the sun's center,
the cardinal's feather.
But sometimes I tire of shading
my eyes. Sometimes, especially
late in the day, the sparrow's
drab is a rest. Now and then
I like to sail an evening lake
with the cold moon for light.
You know I won't be long.
I always return to you
and the flesh.

After Choosing Against Them

Babies are growing on vines
above my window, their fat bottoms
drooping like grapes, sweeter
than summer. I fall in love again,
whispering nursery rhymes as I
pull off my clothes.
Sailboats are rigged with diapers;
as I drift off to where
blue sky meets water
they billow like the cheeks of cherubs.
I know how crazy this is. But
under the giddy lights I felt
my blooming body
release its dreams to the wind.
All over the fields of South Carolina
my milkweed children drift.
As far away as Charleston
their names disturb the air.

A Bargain at Any Price

Daily I go to the carpet warehouse.
The men think I can't make up my mind.
But the truth is, I have fallen in love
with the young ex–football player
who lights the dingy room with his hair.
Even machines can't help him add,
so we spend hours figuring and refiguring
costs—pad and labor, stairs and tax,
his patient golden head bent over the numbers,
the muscles in his arms reflecting shadows
like water under summer clouds.
Each time he starts the motor on the forklift,
slowly pushing that long steel rod
into the center of a roll, then
lifting it out for me to see, Oh—
it's as if an inner sky were opening,
and all his hazy calculations
fall like stars into my heart.

Country Living

Teaching the ducks independence,
I'll tell you, isn't easy.
We have other work to do.

And sifting through the oats
all day, riding the wagon—
they can't fool us into believing
it means the world is golden.

Even beans
take delicate fingers,
and the raspberries cling
to their old ways
no matter who goes in.

But when the tall corn
resists the wind,
holding onto its sweetness
like well-brought-up girls,
there's a certain pride
you can claim.

Who'd give up shelling peas,
fat secrets
spilling into a pure white pan?

All I Ever Wanted Was a God

        I keep trying to be Leda,
        but no one presses his feathers
        hard on my thighs; no one
        catches my hair in his beak,
        pulling me hot through the sky.
        Nobody even gets jealous
        of the birds I keep caged.
        I'd like to pretend indifference,
        but the ponds of my dreams
        keep filling with swans,
        and my rationalizations—
                the men I've loved rarely
                had hollow bones, and
                Olympians frequently make
                bad husbands, and who, after all,
                would really want Helen
                for a daughter
        just sound like sour grapes.

All My Orifices Are Too Small

You laugh when I tell you, but it is truth.
Countless physicians have affirmed it, according
to their various specialties. The oral surgeon,
removing my five wisdom teeth (yes, there really
were five. Some people, he said, grow eight,
two where normal people have one, upper and lower,
right and left. My extra one was upper left)
remarked that my mouth was extraordinarily small.
Friends snickered, but I had known for some time.
A grinning orthodontist, when I was twelve, insisted
that my oral cavity would not accommodate everything
necessary, and he removed four large and perfectly
healthy canines. And then there have been the matters
of ears and nose, so easily irritated by the tiniest
foreign matter. Oh the hours I've spent draining
those narrow tubes. Though delicacy prevents my going
into detail, hemorrhoids are another
manifestation. Gynecologists, too, acknowledged
that a head would be hard pressed to make it through *that*
passage. And they were right. The alternative
was not entirely pleasant, and I no longer wear
bikinis, but there are obvious compensations.
Some of us will do anything to assert our
individuality. I do not maintain, of course,
that these problems are totally distinctive, but
you will have to admit, my claim is somewhat unique.

Trying to Change the Subject

I have sworn to quit
inviting antelope
and elk
into my small back yard,
but the bear refuses
to stop wandering in.
His fur
always gets caught
in the gate
and his steps
on the porch
rattle the glasses
in my cupboard.
Each time he comes
the dog is nervous
for a week.
When he ate my blackberries
I said it didn't matter
but in fact
I had nothing to eat
all day. Yet
when I tell him
I've decided against him,
he laughs,
batting my wind chimes
with his paw.

Alliances

>   *Richard!* your mother called, and you
>   scrambled down from the tree house
>   or jumped from the swing
>   like a pilot bailing out. When your father
>   left, her hands were always empty,
>   so you brought her apples, maple leaves,
>   cups of lemon tea. *Yes,*
>   you said over and over, *yes,*
>   seeing her swollen eyes in the mornings.
>
>   Now they come to visit
>   and you talk with him for hours
>   of your mother, your wife,
>   who glance uneasily in
>   as the two of you drink
>   by the dwindling light. At last
>   you confess the sin
>   that blooms in your nights,
>   and he nods, remembering that dark flower.
>   Forgiveness flushes you both like wine.
>
>   The women could be sisters.
>   In the next room, laying the Sunday table,
>   they share your betrayals like jewelry,
>   each offering the other her heaviest,
>   most expensive stone.

Listening

All night he listens. When she dreams,
her lips part, sometimes she nearly speaks.
But he does not hear the sharp
intake of breath that might mean she knows
a woman has entered their bedroom again,
has passed between them
like a gust of wind, quickening his heartbeat,
disrupting the air.
At breakfast her gestures seem strained,
he can't be sure. He wishes she'd turn
on him suddenly, waving a letter,
secrets exploding from each page,
filling the kitchen with smoke.
But the morning is like
any other, except when she says his name,
it sounds like a prayer.

Deceptions

Ben isn't in his room.
Your mother's impatient voice calls you
down from the attic, where you've
been reading, listening to the rain.
You know it isn't your brother
she's worried about, or you,
but you pull your slicker on and go out
to look for him, to please her.
Today she won't mention your father,
who's been gone since Friday this time,
hunting, farther north. He told her
when the ducks fly over it's like
an arrow through the sun—the whole world
divides. He told you a man can shoot
and miss so easily he almost believes
he loves them better flying.
He never brings one home, and though
your mother seems to mind, you're glad.
You don't like to imagine soft bodies,
stiffened wings. This weekend, even
before he left, the sun had disappeared.
Your mother thinks of the cold dawns,
the rain, the empty blind.

Fear in New Hampshire

    I had forgotten how snow
    darkens the day, the gray sky
    lowering until you think
    the trees may disappear.
    This morning, walking to the cabin,
    strains of organ music,
    a half-familiar hymn, filtered
    through the woods
    as if some ghostly ceremony
    had to be played out.
    Now I listen to the rising wind,
    a log burning itself out
    quietly, in the fireplace.

    Later your voice on the phone
    will assure me this life is real.
    But I could be convinced
    the past is settling over me
    like a shroud, and you,
    and the South, and love
    are the last feverish dreams.

Your Letter

I want a balloon of white birds
flying straight up from dark trees—
you give me a report on your taxes.
I look for silk scarves
tucked among your words
like violets in a picnic basket,
but there is only the zucchini
ripening in your garden.
When I think of your house,
its secret desires—
sheets smelling of oranges,
a wish for my hand on the bannister,
I am lonely as a child again.
Stars light this mountain sky
like kisses, so distant
they are abstractions,
nothing like love.

How Many Women Do You Pass Each Day?

Yesterday I watched you
from the corner, from behind
the newsstand, watched as you ran
to catch up with a red-haired woman
who turned out to be the daughter
of your dentist, a girl with eyes
blue as a Siamese cat's—
not mine. Later you climbed
the stairs to your office, caught
sight of someone getting on
the elevator, dark skirt swirling in,
who could almost have been me,
and ran three flights, but missed her,
your breath when you came back down
short as the greeting you gave
the stranger waiting by your door.
I've considered whether to hide
in your closet, to surprise you
like a gift left ostentatiously
on your desk. But I keep thinking
how you like to discover everything
for yourself—the years it takes
to decide a fate, old songs
on the radio, routes through poems
and beds and snow.

Trying to Make Light of Our Loneliness

for Stella

We reminisce about love
the way our mothers recall
that picnic on the Red Cedar
just before a tornado bruised the sky.
They'd never been so excited,
so pleased the world could turn plum
in a moment, such furious air
could leave them whole.

Our pasts deliver up prizes
the way the cat leaves shimmering
snakes on the doorstep.
I tell you about the man
with the green silk shorts,
you give me the faithless bisexual.
We laugh, remembering other disguises
men shed like skins.

We do not share our own transformations,
lovers who broke up our winters,
making us quick streams.
You smile, wave to dismiss
some private thought,
I think of the man I still love,
the mass of hair on his chest,
my hands in it,
his heart an anxious bird
against my palms.

Things We Can't Prepare For

The end of the affair. His eyes
come back when you're driving,
startle you from the rearview mirror,
his hands stay on your skin
the way trees brush the side
of a barn, their shadows permanent
as the sun fades paint around them.

The death of a brother, whose whistle
still pierces the air, electric,
waking you from sound sleep,

or a child's growth into manhood,
the sudden gesture that makes him
his father, the way he taps the newspaper,
straightening it,
how he lowers his eyes.

A fear that your life is narrowing
to the town, the street you'll choose
next, a dark house where love
will be a small vacation, a month
at most, when you'll neglect the yard.

The Wisdom

Find the island. You will know it
for the shore is too rocky for landings
and a yellow flag waves from the peak
of its one small mountain. Go there
by balloon. The balloon must be striped
and of many colors. I have seen
the perfect one floating near
my house. We can find its owner
together, and he will give it
gladly. When you land
use the silk for adornment.
You will not need a house or a hut
or clothing, for the weather is perfect
always. And when one evening you hear
the voices of children, I will come.
We will begin to discover
the wisdom, to create the seasons.

LIBRARY OF DAVIDSON COLLEGE

Books on regular loan may be checked o
must be presented at the Circulation